# The Riverbend Eagle Tree
# A Bully In The Nest

JULENE BAILIE

Copyright © 2016 Julene Bailie

All rights reserved.

ISBN: 069281857X
ISBN-13: 978-0692818572

## DEDICATION

To my family, Collin (my little eagle and editor), and to my Fellow Eagle Watchers.

## CONTENTS

|    | Prologue | i |
|----|----------|---|
| 1  | The New Nest | 3 |
| 2  | The Eggs | 7 |
| 3  | Hungry in the Nest | 14 |
| 4  | A Bully in the Nest | 18 |
| 5  | Daily Nest Routine | 31 |
| 6  | Eaglet Down | 78 |
| 7  | Brother to the Rescue | 120 |
| 8  | Bald Eagle FAQs | 132 |
| 9  | Bullying | 134 |
| 10 | Acknowledgements | 135 |

## PROLOGUE

In the summer of 2014, the Riverbend Eagle nest collapsed before the eaglets were old enough to fly. The eaglets survived and their story was told in the book, "The Eagle Tree". After the 2014 eaglets left to go explore their expanding world, the Riverbend Eagles built a new nest in the tree next to the old nest tree. "Bully in the Nest" is Part I of the dramatic story of the Riverbend Eagles from the 2015 nesting season.

# 1 THE NEW NEST

After the old nest that was in the Riverbend Eagle Tree collapsed, mama and papa eagle worked hard to bring leaves, branches, sticks, and grass into the tree to build a new nest. They started building in the fall of 2014, and finished in the spring of 2015. Just in time to start a new family.

JULENE BAILIE

When the nest was finished, mama and papa sat in the nest tree and talked about how hard they worked to make the new nest, and how happy they were that it was done.

It was a strong and sturdy nest, hidden in a large cottonwood tree. Do you see the nest in the tree?

# 2 THE EGGS

When spring began, mama laid our eggs in the nest. Either she or papa eagle had to sit on the eggs for 35 days straight. This was so the eggs would stay warm enough for us to grow inside of them. Sometimes, it would get really hot sitting on the eggs. Mama eagle would breathe through her mouth to try to stay cool.

When mama got too hot, and needed a break, she would tell papa eagle it was his turn to keep the eggs warm. They would trade places in the nest.

Papa took turns sitting on the nest. When one of them was sitting on the nest, the other would go and eat, get cleaned up, and then come back to the nest - just in case the other one needed a break.

Day and night, and night and day, for about 35 days, mama and papa took turns sitting on the eggs.

Then, on April 27th, 2015, mama said, "Papa, come and see! Our chicks are hatching!"

Papa came and looked into the nest, and saw my sister and me breaking out of our eggs. "I think we have a boy and a girl!" He was so happy and proud!

Even though we were now out of our eggs, mama or papa still had to sit on us to keep us warm until our little eaglet bodies could stay warm on our own.

After we hatched, mama and papa had to make sure we stayed safe. So they always kept a look out for any trouble, and never left us alone.

## 3 HUNGRY IN THE NEST

Soon after we hatched, we told mama and papa we were hungry! Now it became their full-time job to keep us fed and safe. Mama or papa would fly out and bring back food for us to eat.

Does your mama or papa bring you food to eat?

After we were a couple of weeks old, we were just strong enough to stand and peek over the top of our nest.

On Mother's Day, May 10, we were almost four weeks old. We got to spend this special day with mama eagle, while papa went out and brought us food.

Mama and papa stayed very busy bringing us food. We were always hungry and would beg for more food. Especially, my sister eagle, who I called "Sissy". As soon as mama or papa would bring food to the nest, Sissy would shove me out of the way so she could eat first.

## 4 A BULLY IN THE NEST

Sissy always pushed herself in front of me so she could eat first. I thought that was very rude.

Sissy wouldn't even let me eat until she was done. I was hungry too, and it did not seem fair that she always got to eat first.

But mama and papa eagle always made sure both of us got enough food to eat, every day.

I thought that Sissy having to eat first might just be a phase. But the very next food delivery, Sissy jumped in front of me again to grab the food before I could.

One time, when mama was preparing our food and wasn't looking, Sissy pecked me in the head! I got really upset and thought my sister was a big bully! I did not like her very much at all.

When I complained about Sissy picking on me, mama eagle flew in and told us that we had better get along, because we were going to be in the nest together for a long time.

I agreed and told sister she should stop being such a bully.

Over time, I learned that no matter what, mama and papa would make sure that both of us had enough food to eat so we could grow up strong and healthy. But it was still annoying that Sissy always had to eat first.

One time, when mama and papa were out of the nest, sister pecked me with her sharp beak! She was a mean sister and I did not like being pecked. I wondered why she was mean to me. I did not understand it. I did not do anything to her, so why was she picking on me?

Does anyone ever pick on you? Or do you ever pick on anyone else? It is not very nice, is it!

When mama saw that Sissy pecked me, and that I was upset, she flew to the nest to talk to us again. Sissy went and hid because she knew she was in trouble, but there was no place to really hide in our nest!

Mama wanted to explain why Sissy was so aggressive and always had to eat first. She told us that female bald eagles were always bigger than male bald eagles, and that in the wild they were always dominant. I asked mama what "dominant" meant, and mama said it meant that female bald eagles are sometimes very bossy or pushy. That is also why Sissy always got to eat first. She said that this was just the way it was with all bald eagle families in the wild. It was to help make sure the females survived so they would have more baby eagles in the future. I asked mama if I was going to survive since I was not a female. She laughed and said of course I would survive, and that Sissy would help me learn how to be a big and strong male eagle. Mama said everyone is different, and that we should try to understand why others behave the way they do. She said it was good we talked about things like this so that we would begin to understand each other better.

After mama left the nest, I kind of understood what she told us but I still did not like it. Sissy and I talked about it too. We wondered if all eagle families were like this, or if it was just the bald eagles. Sissy said she was sorry and did not mean to be a bully.

The more I thought about it, the more things started to make sense. Mama was bigger than papa, and he always let mama eat first even if he was the one who brought food into the nest. Maybe I would talk to papa about this later. Maybe Sissy was not a bully after all!

## 5 DAILY NEST ROUTINE

Each day, Sissy and I had certain things we would do. We woke up, stretched our wings, pooped, practiced things we learned, played, exercised, hollered for food, watched mama and papa, ate, pooped again, played some more, slept, and grew. We did the same things almost every day. This was our routine.

Do you have a daily routine? What are the things you do every day?

One of the things Sissy and I learned was how to help keep our nest clean by pooping over the edge of the nest. We would back up to the edge of the nest and shoot the poop out over the side. We had to be very careful so we didn't back up too far, or we could fall out of the nest.

We would holler for food when we got hungry. Mama or papa would fly to go find us something to eat.

At feeding time, mama or papa would always feed Sissy first, and then would bring food over and feed me. I just learned to be patient and to stay out of Sissy's way until she was finished eating. This worked very well and Sissy did not peck me anymore.

We ate the food that mama and papa brought to the nest. Sometimes we had fish they caught in the Green River that was right under our tree. Sometimes we had chicken or duck. We even had rabbit or other smaller birds. But we really liked the fish!

What is your favorite food?

Mama brought us a really big fish one day! This fish filled up the whole family!

Life in the nest went on. We started paying attention to things happening outside of our nest too.

We saw people watching us so we watched them too. Mama and papa called them the "eagle watchers" and told us they watched over our eagle family to make sure nothing bad happened to us.

We had some excitement in our nest every once in a while too. One day, mama was on the branch babysitting us, and papa brought a small fish to the nest.

Mama was hungry, and she saw papa was going to eat some of the fish. Mama said, "papa, you need to wait until I eat before you eat, remember?"

Papa must have been really hungry or didn't hear what mama said because he and mama had a squabble over who was going to eat the fish first. Sissy and I just stayed out of their way!

Papa moved over to the edge of the nest and let mama eat. Then I remembered what mama told us when she came and talked to Sissy and me about female bald eagles always getting to eat first. This time papa had to wait his turn! I wasn't the only one that had to wait for food. Papa did too! I guess that is just the way it is in a bald eagle's nest.

Mama or papa eagle stayed near our nest all the time. One of them would fly off to take a bath or get us food, and the other would babysit until they came back to the nest. It must have been hard work because sometimes they would take a nap when sister and I were sleeping too.

We learned about other things too. There were some black birds that would come and bother mama and papa. They would dive at them when they were sitting in our tree.

The black birds would also chase mama or papa around when they were flying, and especially if they were bringing food back to the nest. Papa told us the black birds were called "crows" and they were pests. But, he told us crows also helped eagles and other birds of prey. The crows would show eagles where there was easy food to get. Like if an animal was dead in the road, the crows would all fly over there to eat. Mama or papa would watch where the crows went, and would fly in and take the meal away from them. That is why the crows didn't like eagles very much.

Mama and papa would fly from our tree down to the river below us, every day.

They drank water and took baths in the river. They washed their beaks, feet, and feathers, and stayed very clean. We were too little to fly so could not go down to the river with them.

Because we ate so well, we grew very fast.

One day mama and Sissy finished eating and went to take a nap. It was just papa and me eating. After we finished, papa said, "See son, I told you we would always have enough food for both of you, so you don't ever need to worry about mama and Sissy eating first."

Papa was right. I never went to bed hungry and my crop always had food in it. I was so full this day I could hardly move. Look how big my crop is!

Do you see my crop? Do you have a crop?

I admired papa. He was so patient with Sissy and me. I wanted to grow up to be just like him someday.

At six weeks old, we were almost half the size of our parents. Our feathers started to look very funny!

Our daily routine was still the same, only now we were practicing lessons and exercising more and more.

We would play and tumble in our nest. But because Sissy was bigger and stronger than me she would always win.

Sometimes if I thought Sissy was playing too rough, I tattled on her. Mama would have to come to the nest and make Sissy settle down. Mama told us we needed to appreciate each other, and our time together in the nest, because someday soon we would be out on our own.

After mama left the nest, Sissy came over to me and told me she was sorry. She said sometimes she forgot that she was bigger and stronger. She said she would try to remember that for the next time we played.

As the summer went on, it got hotter and drier, and we got bigger…

…and bigger. Our daily routine continued. We woke up, stretched, pooped, learned, played, exercised, ate, pooped again, observed, played some more, slept, and grew.

It seemed like everything Sissy and I did turned into a competition. We even tried to see who could shoot the poop the farthest from the nest!

Sometimes we did our own thing. On this day, Sissy played with a feather while I preened my feathers. Preening was another thing we learned to do and had to practice.

We practiced things we learned from watching mama and papa. I pretended to build a nest because someday when I grow big like papa, I will have to build a nest too!

Mama and papa insisted we exercise our wings every day. Our feathers really started growing out and our wings were getting much, much bigger.

Even though we were old enough to eat on our own, mama would still come into the nest and feed us sometimes. We liked it when mama fed us.

We think mama liked feeding us too. She kept telling us we were growing up too fast.

It was getting harder to exercise in the nest because we were getting so big. Mama and papa spent more and more of their time in the branches or out flying around. One day, Sissy just started wing-flapping me in the head! She still irritated me sometimes.

Sissy asked mama when we would be able to fly. Mama told her it would still be a couple of weeks before we would be strong enough to try to fly. She said to keep exercising and practicing with our wings, and to do our branch hopping because practice made perfect.

Does your mama or papa ever tell you to practice something? What kinds of things do you practice?

Even though we stayed busy with our daily routine, we were both getting a little tired of being cooped up in the nest.

The only way we figured we would get out of the nest is if we learned to fly. So we kept practicing with our wings.

Things were going really good in the nest. Until the day papa brought in a snack and Sissy grabbed it. She mantled over it so I could not get any. This was another thing mama and papa taught us and said that we needed to practice. However, Sissy did not need to practice mantling because she was already good at grabbing food and eating first! I needed to practice mantling too!

But this time Sissy took her practicing a little too far. She stood up and said, "It's all mine!" And then she turned and took the food to the bottom of the nest.

I was really upset and yelled, "I am SO ready to be out of this nest and away from my sister!"

I was mad and wished my Sissy would just go away. I went over to the other side of the nest and pouted.

But then Sissy did something very unexpected. She brought the food over to me and asked if I wanted to share it with her. I could not believe it! My sister wanted to share food with me! Sissy said she realized it was not very nice to take the food like that.

We weren't all that hungry, because we had been getting so many food deliveries to the nest. So, Sissy and I played with the food. We played tug of war and then both ate some of the food together. We laughed and were having fun. I guess she wasn't such a bad sister after all.

But papa saw us playing with our food. Before papa flew into the nest, Sissy laid on the food and hid it from papa. Papa told Sissy and me that he and mama worked really hard to keep us fed, and that we should not play with our food.

Sissy told papa she was sorry, that she and I were just trying to have fun before we shared the snack. Papa seemed a little surprised that Sissy was willing to share her food.

At the end of June and into July, the weather turned really hot, and there hadn't been any rain for days. We would sit with our wings out to try to stay cool. We learned this trick by watching mama and papa. We didn't exercise much in the heat.

# 6 EAGLET DOWN

The weather cooled off a bit one day, and I felt really energized. I decided to exercise and started flapping my wings.

I jumped and hopped, and hopped and jumped all around Sissy.

Sissy looked at me and asked, "Aren't you going a little bit crazy brother?"

I told Sissy I was feeling really good and wanted to practice my wings when it was not so hot out. I wanted to keep practicing so I could leave our hot nest.

Sissy told me to stop. But I hopped, then jumped, and then hopped some more! I was beginning to feel the wind under my wings, and it felt awesome!

I told Sissy she should practice too if she ever wanted to leave the hot nest. And, that I could feel wind in my wings.

Sissy got up and stretched her wings. She said she wanted to feel the wind under her wings too.

Sissy told me she could jump higher than I did. I told her to go ahead and try!

So Sissy started jumping all around the nest. She jumped higher, and higher!

Sissy did jump higher than me! Her feet weren't even touching the nest! I told her to be careful. But she didn't listen and kept jumping, and jumping some more.

In the meantime, mama and papa watched us from the tree where they were resting and trying to stay cool. Mama told papa she was exhausted from all the work they were doing to keep us fed and happy. Papa told mama not to worry, that he heard us talking about feeling the wind in our wings. This was a sign that we would be ready to fly soon.

Sissy finally quit jumping. I told her she better be careful when jumping like that or she might fall out of the nest.

I decided to show off my jumping skills and was going to try to jump higher than Sissy. "Sissy! Watch me!"

When I finished jumping, Sissy looked at me and told me she thought I did pretty good! But that she could jump even better than me.

Sissy got ready to jump. She jumped and flapped her big wings.

Sissy got a little crazy with her hopping and jumping, and was yelling, "I can feel wind in my wings. Wheeee!"

"Wheee! Look at me, brother!"

I got out of Sissy's way. Then, Sissy went to the back of the nest still flapping her wings, and fell right out of the nest! All I could do was watch her fall! Oh, NO!

I couldn't see Sissy anymore, but could hear her falling through branches and leaves. She ended up falling into the lower branches of our tree.

Papa heard Sissy fall and yelled to her, "I'm coming! Stay where you are!"

And papa quickly flew through the tree to go see if Sissy was O.K.

Sissy fell way down in the tree. I didn't know what to do. I was scared!

Sissy fell about 30 feet from the nest. That was a long way down!

Papa flew down into the tree. He looked through the leaves and saw that Sissy was not hurt, but she was sure scared. I think papa was scared too!

Once papa saw that Sissy was not hurt, he told her to stay still and rest. She had to save her strength because she was going to have to climb back up into the nest.

Sissy was tough, and papa said she would be O.K. so I did not worry. I sat on the nest branch and teased her, trying to make her laugh. I told her she fell into the poop cellar, but she did not think that was very funny.

I woke up the next morning, and Sissy wasn't there. I had the whole nest to myself! I preened my feathers and didn't have anyone to bother me. It was kind of nice for a change. I went on with my daily routine, and figured Sissy would be back up in the nest in no time.

The next day, I climbed up onto the nest branch and called for Sissy. She answered quietly, saying she was a little bit scared. I still wasn't worried. She was my big Sissy and would probably come back to the nest very soon. I told her to quit kidding around and to come back up to the nest.

While I waited for Sissy to come back to the nest, I decided to enjoy my alone time. It was awesome! I ate without having to wait. I brushed my beak and no one tried to bite my tail feathers. But, I was bored without Sissy in the nest, and was starting to miss her.

I also used my time alone to practice my branch-hopping skills.

Papa and mama flew around the nest every day and talked to Sissy. They encouraged her to try to climb back up to the nest. They even flew by with food to try to make her fly.

Sissy said she was afraid to move. She was afraid she would fall all the way to the ground. And so she just sat there alone in the lower branches.

When I woke up on the third day, and Sissy was still not back in the nest, I began to worry. Even though I liked having mama and papa and the nest to myself, I started to wonder if Sissy would make it back up to the nest.

I could tell mama and papa were worried too. Everyone was worried about Sissy, even the eagle watchers.

On the fourth day after Sissy fell, papa said that he and mama had tried everything they could think of to get Sissy to climb back to the nest. I tried talking with Sissy but she would not even answer. I got so sad, I only ate a little bit of food that papa brought to the nest. I didn't even feel like brushing my beak after I ate. I missed my Sissy.

Later, I had an idea. What if I was the one to fly by Sissy and try to get her to come back to the nest! I had been practicing my wings all week, and had been practicing my branch hopping too! Maybe I could fly if I really tried. I had to do something to get my Sissy back. Even though she picked on me and teased me and always got to eat first, she was not a bully. She was my sister! I had to try to save her.

I asked papa what he thought about the idea.

Papa and mama talked about the idea of me flying down to Sissy. Mama was worried she would have two eaglets stuck down in the tree. Papa said he had been watching me branch hop and practice my wings. He felt I was ready to fly. They both agreed they were out of other options.

Papa flew closer to me and said, "Son, your idea just might work! But you are going to have to be careful. We don't want you getting stuck down there too." I told papa not to worry.

Papa flew around the tree to one of the lower branches closer to Sissy. He hollered out to me, "Son, you need to fly around the tree and land in here where I am". And then he flew out to make room for me.

I told papa O.K., and yelled out to Sissy, "Don't worry Sissy, I am coming to get you!"

All of the eagle watchers were out watching us that day. They were worried about Sissy too, but there was nothing they could do to help her. Humans can not interfere with eagles in the wild.

Mama closed her eyes. She couldn't bear to watch what was going to happen next.

# 7 BROTHER TO THE RESCUE

I told mama not to worry, that I would be fine. I went up to the edge of the launching branch and started flapping my wings. I flapped them faster and harder. Suddenly, my big wings lifted me off the branch so that my feet were not touching anymore! I was scared but my wings took over. I just kept telling myself to keep flapping, keep flapping, keep flapping!

And I flew!!!! I flew around the nest tree to the place that papa showed me.

I landed on the branch above where Sissy was. She saw me fly in and she could not believe it! I could not believe it either! It was scary, but it was also fun! I had to sit and catch my breath for a minute. Then, I had to focus on helping Sissy get back to the nest.

I asked Sissy how she felt. She said she was getting really tired of being in the poop cellar, and was really hungry. That was the Sissy I knew – always thinking about food. Sissy couldn't believe I flew to save her. She thought I did not like her because she was mean to me. I told her that I didn't like some of the things she did, but that she was my sister and I loved her and missed her. Sissy said she loved me too, and that she missed being with me in the nest.

We decided to make getting back to the nest a game of branch hopping. I told Sissy I wouldn't leave without her, and all she had to do was follow me up the branches. So that's what she did! We hopped one branch at a time until we made it all the way up the tree and back to our nest! All of my practice with my wings and branch hopping paid off.

Mama and papa eagle couldn't believe it! After four days with no food, and in the heat of the summer, Sissy survived and was back in the nest! They said she was one lucky eagle to have a brother like me. Mama was so relieved! Both of her eaglets were back in the nest, safe and sound.

When we made it back to the nest, Sissy told me that she was so happy to have a brave brother like me. She didn't know what she would have done if I hadn't helped her climb back to the nest.

We were both exhausted from our branch hopping and climbing back to the nest. We laid down, happy to be back together.

Papa went right out and brought food back for us. I knew Sissy was super hungry and I let her eat, and eat some more. This was the first time ever that I was happy that Sissy got to eat first.

The next day, I was so excited to have Sissy back with me in the nest. I wanted to get back to our daily routine, and wanted to play and fly some more! I told her about all the fun things I had been doing. Sissy said she was really tired and didn't feel like doing anything. I continued flying around the tree, practicing how to take-off and land. Sometimes I would fly with papa and mama. But Sissy wouldn't leave the nest.

I was learning how to hunt, and even went down to the river with papa one day and took a bath. I was so excited! I would come back to the nest and tell Sissy about my adventures and what I was learning. I wanted her to come with me, but all she wanted to do was stay in the nest. This was not the big, strong, bold Sissy I knew. Something was wrong.

About a week after Sissy came back to the nest, papa came and talked to her. He told her she was old enough to fly now, and that she needed to keep exercising her wings, and practicing her branch hopping. She should also try to fly.

Sissy looked up at papa and quietly said, "But papa, I am afraid to fly. What if I fall again?"

## TO BE CONTINUED…

The 2015 nesting season drama continues in the next book, "The Eaglet Who Wouldn't Fly", to be published in early 2017. Find out what happens to Sissy and her brother. Does Sissy overcome her fear of flying? Does she leave the nest? What happens to her brother? All of these questions, and more, will be answered in the continuing saga of The Riverbend Eagles.

Can't wait for Spring for more Riverbend Eagle photos and stories? Join us in our journey in watching this eagle family.

Join our "Fellow Eagle Watchers" group on Facebook
See Ralph's videos on YouTube – RHM Sheeprugly
See group photos on flickr – Riverbend Eagles

# BALD EAGLE FREQUENTLY ASKED QUESTIONS

In the first book about the Riverbend Eagles, "The Eagle Tree", we listed some frequently asked questions (FAQs) that we hear from children and adults that pass by the Riverbend eagle tree. Below are some more questions and answers we thought you would like.

**Q: How do you tell the difference between a male and female bald eagle?**
**A:** With the Riverbend Eagle pair, that is easy! Papa eagle has a dark dot on his head. However, this isn't really how you can tell the difference in all bald eagles. The main difference is their size. Female bald eagles are bigger than the male. There are other ways to tell the difference too.
(see https://www.learner.org/jnorth/tm/eagle/ExpertAnswer06.html - Q&A with Peter Nye in 2006, New York Department of Environmental Conservation)

**Q: What temperature do eagle eggs need to be incubated at?**
**A:** Eagle eggs need to be maintained at a temperature near 105 degrees Fahrenheit (40 degrees Celsius) for between 34 and 36 days.

**Q: Do bald eagles see in black and white, or color?**
**A:** Bald eagles see in color. Their eyesight is quite good during the daytime, but not as good at night.

**Q: What is the eagle's favorite food?**
**A:** Although eagles eat lots of different things, their most favorite food is fish.

**Q: Do bald eagles have any natural predators?**
**A:** Bald eagles do not have very many natural predators. Besides humans, only a few large birds of prey, such as large owls, and mammals like raccoons are a threat to the bald eagle. Other eagles can be threats as well.

**Q: How tall is an adult bald eagle?**
**A:** An adult bald eagle stands about 30 inches tall.

**Q: How do eagles regulate their body temperature?**
**A:** Eagles control their body temperature, called "thermoregulation", by panting with their mouth open, or through heat loss through their legs and feet, which do not have feathers.

**Q: Why do the bald eagles have white heads?**
**A:** No one really knows for sure, but there are a couple of probable reasons. One is that it is a sign of maturity, so it shows age. Another is so that eagles can tell the difference between different eagle species.

**Q: In the story, we saw the eagle had a very large crop. What is a crop?**
**A:** A crop, on a bird, is an expandable pouch, made of muscle located near the gullet or throat. The purpose for the crop is to store excess food for later digestion.

**Q: Where do the eaglets go when they leave the nest?**
**A:** When I "Googled" this question, the answer I got was, "Studies show that juveniles are generally nomadic in the first four years of their life and can cover extensive geographic areas. The studies also show that when the juveniles are ready to mate, they tend to return to the general area where they were born. If a juvenile attempted to return to its birth nest, the adult pair would drive them away as they would any intruding eagle." Source - https://www.nationaleaglecenter.org/eagle-nesting-young/.

## BULLYING

During the 2015 nesting season, we observed 'bullying' behavior in the Riverbend eagle nest. This book talks about sister eagle bullying her brother eagle, and they end up working things out in the story. Unfortunately, for too many children and young adults bullying is a serious matter that, if not addressed, may cause physical or emotional damage.

I encourage anyone who feels they are being bullied, or if you think you are a bully, to talk to an adult about the situation. Don't feel you have to deal with the situation on your own. Ask for help. There are so many options available, some of which I've listed below.

People you trust and can talk to and ask for help:

- Parents, grandparents, aunts or uncles, or extended family members
- Teachers
- School counselors
- A church pastor

For more information on what you can do if you or someone you know is being bullied, or if you think you are a bully, there are a number of websites that offer help and suggestions. I've listed just a few of these below.

- https://www.stopbullying.gov/
- http://kidshealth.org/en/parents/bullies.html
- http://www.helpguide.org/articles/abuse/dealing-with-bullying.htm

# ACKNOWLEDGEMENTS

To my family – immediate and extended. Thank you all for your support and encouragement. I transitioned from the crazy cat lady to the crazy eagle lady, and you still accept me as I am (I think). Nephew Collin Anderson – thank you for your 'eagle eye' in editing the book and for being my first reader.

Ralph Meier, my mentor, raptor specialist, and friend. Thank you for educating me and the other Fellow Eagle Watchers about eagle behavior, and for your endless stories about bird behavior (and other topics). I am eternally grateful for our paths crossing at the Riverbend eagle tree.

For the original "Fellow Eagle Watchers" – the group of professional photographers and videographers who started hanging out at the tree – Ralph, the two Steve's, Ken, Debbie, Bob, Jeffrey, Vicki, Simon, Gary, Kimberley, and Peter. Thank you for your fellowship, friendship, inspiration, advice, laughs, entertainment, and adventures at the eagle tree and beyond.

Contributing photographers Steven Arvid Gerde and Ralph Meier. Thank you for your photographs and video excerpts that captured the eagles in moments that I needed to complete the story.

To Jim Raymond and Ken Morain for your expertise in making my "not so professional" photos more book-worthy.

To all the new additions to the ever growing group of Fellow Eagle Watchers. Your enthusiasm for photography, nature, and the eagles inspires me to continue writing the Riverbend Eagle Tree stories.

And to mama and papa eagle for letting us observe them in the wild. We love our Riverbend Eagle family who have touched more lives than they could ever know.

www.ingramcontent.com/pod-product-compliance
Lightning Source LLC
Chambersburg PA
CBHW042033150426
43201CB00002B/14